Jim Emerton

MORE PiECES OF JiM EMERTON

FURTHER MUSINGS AND ORIGINAL OBSERVATIONS
ON NATURE, MAN AND THE UNIVERSE

Jim Emerton

MORE PiECES OF JiM EMERTON

FURTHER MUSINGS AND ORIGINAL OBSERVATIONS
ON NATURE, MAN AND THE UNIVERSE

MEREO
Cirencester

Mereo Books

1A The Wool Market Dyer Street Cirencester Gloucestershire GL7 2PR
An imprint of Memoirs Publishing www.mereobooks.com

More pieces of Jim Emerton: 978-1-86151-661-9

First published in Great Britain in 2016
by Mereo Books, an imprint of Memoirs Publishing

The address for Memoirs Publishing Group Limited can be found at
www.memoirspublishing.com

The Memoirs Publishing Group Ltd Reg. No. 7834348

The Memoirs Publishing Group supports both The Forest Stewardship Council®
(FSC®) and the PEFC® leading international forest-certification organisations. Our
books carrying both the FSC label and the PEFC® and are printed on FSC®-certified
paper. FSC® is the only forest-certification scheme supported by the leading
environmental organisations including Greenpeace. Our paper procurement policy
can be found at www.memoirspublishing.com/environment

Typeset in 8.5/12pt Century Schoolbook
by Wiltshire Associates Publisher Services Ltd. Printed and bound in Great Britain
by Printondemand-Worldwide, Peterborough PE2 6XD

MIX
Paper from
responsible sources
FSC
www.fsc.org   FSC® C004959

CONTENTS

I

NATURE AND THE OUTDOORS

Nature is the living god
Forms us, shapes and takes us
There is no start, no finish
Its power will never diminish
Wise man does not bother
He knows his centre, the Earth Mother
The death of a spider, firefly burned
Great wheel of life is always turned

THE HOUSEBOAT

Moored deep on remote wash saltings
Lifted by spring tides of the North Sea
My imagination soared above reality
A young boy alone on the sea
Only mist, seals, iodine and salt joined me
The Tilley lamp flickered as the air ran out
Not a wildfowler would hear my shout
Of a lonely youth intoxicated
By earthly elements
And life itself.

WILDERNESS

Ice crystals cling to my face
The foaming tide, fluffed with salt
Creeps around my feet
Seals calling from lonely sandbanks
Of the North Sea washes
An eerie, plaintive curlew cry
The sound resonating with each tingling sensation
At one with ancient and eternal wash elements

The snowflakes, driven by Arctic wind

Burning my face with a sweet embrace

Alone in my uniqueness

Tasting the joy of nature's freedom

Urged on by primal instincts

Into heady and sublime euphoria

The purity of spirit

United at last.

COUNTRY BOY'S DREAM

Absorbed, detached in silent contemplation

Orange sensations of trellised and cherished nasturtiums

Flood my brain

Butterflies dancing over buddleia blooms

Alert to every emerging snowdrop bloom

The wonder of shiny blue eggs

Nestling on the firm but soft mud of a song thrush nest

An excited climb up ancient yew

To marvel at the mossy greenfinch nest

Wild geese grazing, alive and alert,

The watching sentinels on the grassy paddock

Bats lured by the twilight sky

To catapulted stones reacting as if to evening moths.

THE SPARROWS

A host of sparrows bathed in snowbound sunshine

Each chirpy soul part of nature's chorus

What little gems are spoken?

A symphony of avian oneness

The symphony of messages, stories and assertions

Humble birds,

Taking their place in the hum
The pulse of life itself
How it inspires my wonder!

THE SNOWDROP

Glistening snowdrop, I watched you grow
Eyes probing the depths below
Winter beauty in petal form
Spirit reaching out to the icy storm
When others shiver, in retreat from cold
a work of art, you are so bold
In the ancient cycle that takes place
Beneath the feet of the human race
 Each perfect bloom
White heart, of nature's bounty.

THE CAT

What is this curiosity
A feline monstrosity?
Master of his domain
Free to roam again
He is cool and aloof
Whilst sitting on the roof
Murderous hunter of wee little mice
Toying and playing within a trice
The dogs they come out barking
Hackles raised, alarming
You cannot probe his furry depths
The cat upon the concrete steps.

THE OLD OAK TREE

Old oak tree, speak to me
Reveal your untold secrets
Of when wolves howled, bears roamed
Sunsets died, storms brewed
And men killed deer beneath ancient boughs
You are the voice of nature
Uniting me with the past
The Sun, the Earth, the icy blast
When machines were mice, and men were lions
Your branches quake
With the weight of ancient times.

DANCE OF THE BUTTERFLIES

Cascading, colliding, freewheeling
As the warm wind buoys their little spirits in a gentle breeze
Above the purple haze of buddleia nectar
They sway and dance in airy iridescence
Only the bird of paradise can hope to match
The pure shimmering beauty of the peacock's wings.
It is the dance of love, of hope
Played out in brief moments of time
And in transient rapture
Long may the artist of nature
Transport my imagination.

THE LIVING GOD

Nature is the living god
Forms us, shapes and takes us
There is no start, no finish
Its power will never diminish
Wise man does not bother
He knows his centre, the Earth Mother
The death of a spider, firefly burned
Great wheel of life is always turned.

BEAUTIFUL DREAMER

In my intuitive eye
I want to fly
To soar above the sky
To sing sweet words of freedom
Unleash a spirit into the arms of euphoria
To cleanse my soul with the feather touch of airy beauty
Take me on a kaleidoscope trip of colours warm and sensual
Feel the wind swirl around my face
Be absorbed in the timeless moment
Empty myself of the dark demon
Emerge from a pupa
A pure imago
Like the butterfly that shines so bright on nature's palate.

MANEATER

In densest shadows, the fiery eyes of panther lurk
A predator, shaped by time to rule the jungle by deathly ambush
We marvel at the savage power
An energy is stirred deep within our psyche

With insight we form a primeval
Connection with this feline killing machine
We are at one with the vibrant force
We call it nature, the womb of all being!

BIRD OF PARADISE

Jewel of the jungle, fill me with rapture
A beauty beyond our capture
Dance like a whirling dervish
Fill the forest, a performing artist
Take your place beneath the sun
Light my life with your heavenly fun
Rest your laurels at nature's bow
You are symbolic, a bird of now.

WATER

The highest good is like water
It dwells in places that men despise
Thus it approaches the tao
Taking life and giving birth
To the riches of the sea
Feeds us, fuels us with nature's elixir
A single drop falls from my skin
To remind me that I am alive today.

THE ROSE

Fragrant cloud, seduce my brain with sultry beauty
You are the image of my youthful innocence
Let me sense once more your sweet perfume
To feel the rush of nature perfect
A sublime moment of sheer delight.

THE BEAR

My senses pierced the bottomless chasm of his eyes
No humanity reflected there
Only primal, cold instinct was perceived
Aeons of pure survival lent a signature
To his essence of being.
We are in symphony, we are one
He left me awestruck with a fearsome sound
As he devoured the honey from my silver spoon
The impact stirred my soul
And raised my spirit in silent admiration.

LAKE DAHL

Drawing deep on the cool smoke from the pipe within
Listening to the burst of each bubble
I entered a trance, and flowed with the emergent spirit
Then the rush of lovely feeling
Dancing in pure ecstasy on a water lily
And somersaulting, touching cool blue
Touching hot red
Soaring over the Himalayas
A free spirit in the earthly sky.

THE FIGHTING COCK

Purest spirit in dominant eye
The banty cock soon would die
Never have I seen the like
A noble savage in avian form
On this earth to rule the roost
And soon to give my ego boost
Never have I seen such fire
The wonder of his mighty eye.

ANNAPURNA

Sweet fragrance from flowers for the bund
Looking up, observing the sky
First white clouds, appeared at the edge of sight
What's the weather like so far?
Then the dawning, the sudden grasp
Feeling small at nature's wonder
The mighty slopes of Annapurna
Moments to transform a life.

THE YETI

I live on snow-clad peaks, one of nature's freaks
Not just a showman
I am the abominable snowman
Dwelling in the mountains.
I drink from streams and fountains
Now I drive you loco
As you try to take my photo
You want to see me clear and crisp
But I am a will o' the wisp
I dwell within the shallows
Behind rocks, trees and shadows
To haunt you with a history
Of folklore, time and mystery.

THE ABYSS

Contemplating a deep-sea world is like a psychic journey
We meet strange and beautiful forms
Confront and face the unknown
Transmuting, changing the alien into reality

A voyage into deep, inner space
The ocean floor is an echo of the self
A trip that unites the very soul.

MISTY MORN WILDFOWLING

The cat tide creeps around my feet
Raindrops, tinged with iodine, cling to my face
Poised in this remote creek
Still within the stalk edges and sea lavender
My eyes pierce the horizon as a lone goose wings a primeval path
Along the saltings of ancient wilderness
This is the hunting ground of the adventurous eccentric
Whose being is heightened by the oneness of nature;
The elements he embraces
The rapture, the unity of mind and senses.

SILVER BIRCH

Delicate leaves caressed by a swaying breeze
A vision of arboreal loveliness
No architect could design your form
As she kisses my eyes
Fires my wonder
And plants her seeds
In the forest of my mind
Uniting me with earthly elements.
Transient moments, I am the tree
We are one.

LOTUS BLOSSOM

The symbol of Indian purity
Sold for one rupee by childish innocence
Beneath the circling vultures
Of the Hindu ashes
An image of pure beauty
In this restless sea of corruption
Water buffalo floating by
Its life absorbed by the sacred river
The rising sun illuminates with a fiery near spiritual glow
A kaleidoscope of images, sights and sounds to transfix my eager psyche.

THE RAVEN

Black gloss on silken plumes
Fresh from dark Satanic shadows
You appear, a primeval phantom in the earthly sky
Flying in with a winged message from ancient folklore
You are the messenger that stirs the essence of mind
That returns us to our primal self
Raise me up, return me to the light of day
Bring me peace again.

MY BIRD TABLE

Red and gold finches on thistle seeds
How they love these weeds
Walking from the back door
A super, fine, black jackdaw
The timid little coal tit
Thrills my mind, feeds my wit
It is nectar to the senses

A sight for us old Mensas
Full of artist's delight
Sparrowhawk created a big fright
In my next reincarnation
My table fires the nation.

THE SWANS

Purest white, in wave after wave
Their dazzling forms sway and glide
In timeless romance
King and queen of the shimmering depths
In ancient dance, a sweet embrace
Moments of wonder
In glistening, reflected gravity
The dance of love
In majestic consummation.

BLACK SWANS

Devil birds that swim in satanic majesty
in the firmament of my inner psyche
Avian harbingers spelling death to the ego
Liberators of spiritual evil.

THE FEATHER

When you gaze up into the sky, a feather may float by. It has fallen from a far off cloud, from the cosmic bird that flew on transcendent wings, to bring a message from the angels. They beckon us to a higher place, where spirits soar above the race which is the curse of material man. When I am born again, the birds of paradise will perform for me, and shape a lovely destiny, as they court and dance on fire with shimmering beauty. The wonders I have seen, the dancing bear, the beauty queen, colour, the patterns I have found at the centre of my mind.

WILD AND FREE

A young spirit, wild and free on a path, escapes from reality. I bathed in the oceans, walked in the woods; in my belief I placed my trust. In the mountain air, with not a care, I soared like an eagle, danced like a dervish and relished all that was good and beautiful. It was good to feel the pulse of the earth and sow the seeds of spiritual rebirth. Bare, stripped back to my naked self, I felt the power of another morph, becoming whole and at one with things that I had seen, touched and felt. Now empowered from a world within, I cast aside my earthly sins.

SURROUNDED BY BEAUTY

I walked out today to be greeted by a host of golden dandelions. The swifts flew high in the sky, symbolic of better days to come. I revelled in the flight of a bumble bee and the sun-kissed tree, glowing wonderful and green. The voice of nature was loud and clear, each bird a sonorous instrument of pure harmony. This feeling should never die, the love so perfect in you and I. In the next life I will be the summer breeze, the snow that falls and the ancient branches of cherished oak. In life on this sweet Earth, I have been blessed by wondrous things and surrounded by beauty.

THIS WARM AND BEAUTIFUL FEELING

I want it all to never die

The lights I see in the sky

When I gaze upon the sun from the nothing I had become.

My eyes were full today, and as the wind blew by I knew I would never die, as a single raindrop trickled down my cheek to shock my senses back to life.

As we flowed along, in the woods of long ago,

I felt the closeness of the earth below

As the orchestra of nature played a summer song

To ease me into the throng

So that I felt at one with time and place

Beyond the pulse of the human race.

One day when the bodily morph is done, I will find my place in the fallen leaves

On the lonely rock in the mountain stream.

WHEN THE NORTH WIND BLOWS

Alone in the wilderness, listening to the voice of nature, I found my place. A walk along the sea wall at night as high as a kite, as the wild duck flew against the scudding clouds, and the short-eared owl hovered above my head. The moon loomed large, shedding its cool, melancholy light, as it shimmered on tidal pools. Curlew, primeval birds of the vast open spaces, filled my ears with plaintive and eerie calls, as ancient remnants of a haunted past. Then the clouds were occluded as the north east wind, fresh from Siberia, stung my face, with snowflakes tinged with iodine from the North Sea. All the books I have read, the things I have seen, do not compare with the raw instincts of pure being.

DANCE OF THE GNATS

In timeless display they emerged on to the stage of spring in an aerial ballet of the insects. The mating ritual began as they cavorted in the warm and gentle air. What wonders the garden has concealed, as the cold winter days marked time. From beneath the fallen leaves, the earth pulsed with life, as the hedgehog stirred, the blackbirds echoed mellifluous notes, all the children of Mother Nature. The dance of the gnats excites me within, as I celebrate another day at one with natural things.

THE SUN AT GOA

I gazed upon the fiery ball, and knew it was all I would see in that part of my destiny. Crows danced and cawed, and flew as shadows against the setting sun. Soaking up the final, soothing rays of another day in paradise, I sensed a sublime feeling, becalmed and serene. I drew deep upon an image that one day would morph into poetry, to re-enact a few precious moments under the intensity of a cosmic flow, that came to show me the spirit of the earth, a living rebirth of all that is fine and beautiful.

I CAME ALIVE IN THE MORNING RAIN

Stepping out in the morning rain, I came alive, as teardrops of the sky refreshed my skin.

The rising spring plants glowed with new life, and my eyes were transfixed by the rosy breast of a bullfinch hiding in the hawthorn.

Again I felt the wonder of the earth, and surrounded by pulses of life, the spirit of it all came to me.

Wild and beautiful places fill me with awe and wonder of the intricate web of life.

Created or evolved, I sense a unity of design and reflect that every creature, great and small just *is*.

THE PRIMITIVE

Alone in wilderness and down to basic instincts, you may have some serious lessons in life. Stripped of formal academic conventions and the popular veneer of society, you gain a sense of stark reality. As a wildfowler in the unforgiving Wash Estuary, I embraced life, death and the wild elements. It is vital to feel the sun, wind, snow and rain on bare skin. A walk along the sea wall under the moon and stars is both eerie and enchanting. I loved a camel ride into the setting sun of the Sahara, as it glistened on whispering white sands. The city slicker in the concrete jungle is alien to the Earth in this primitive sense. Everyman should explore the freedom that the true primitive feels.

THE DELIGHTS OF SPRING

The world is alive with the orchestra of nature, the notes being played in yonder glade where the swallows flit, and the pheasant sits in plumes of emerald splendour. The daffodils dazzle in the warming rays, as the wind nods their gentle heads in harmony and agreement, to make it clear that the Earth has burst into life. I love to flow in spiritual glow along the mountain stream, where the fish glimmer and teem, as the spectre of the grey heron casts its deathly shadow over the waters deep. Each tiny ray of a diffused sun is the harbinger of new life yet to come, as the animals are courting in the enchanting early morning. It has been a lovely day at one and in the arms of sweet nature.

I WENT OUT FOR A WALK TODAY

I went for a walk today, to kill the ghosts of yesterday.

My senses were filled by the rush of spring, the clear blue sky with buzzards high, as sparring robins disguised their real intentions with sweet courtship songs.

The troglodyte caressed my ears with a shrill and busy little song, as I came alive in the wooded glade, no more the urban shade, but into the sun where rabbits searched in the fallen leaves, where ancient oaks had shed nature's fruits.

I felt at one with each step in time of a single man, absorbed within the earthly shrine of sweet nature.

ANIMAL AND BIRD COMMUNICATION IN NATURE

As a keen lover and student of the world of nature, I have observed many animals in the wild and seen how they behave towards other birds and other species. It is apparent to my human mind that many respond to each other through visible behaviours and sounds. A deciduous wood is like a huge interconnected lifeform. Just observe when a feral cat, fox of bird of prey makes an appearance and listen to the mutual exchange of alarm calls. What is our understanding of this language, how has it evolved over time, which are the key player species in the orchestra of nature? How do we analyse this natural phenomenon on a human psychological level, with or without anthropomorphisms? Perhaps it may be valuable to perceive nature as one united entity - this may have intuitive value to the human psyche. Even with empathy, absolute reality in this sense must be beyond our scope as mere humans.

ANIMALS, BIRDS AND MAN IN CONCERT

I look upon the pulse of life that radiates from far and wide. I fear the lion, sense the mouse and see the bat above my house. In all the wonders that I hear and see is a timeless symmetry. Beyond the scope and reach of man, in one single earthly span, I feel the spirit of each living form, the bird that sings until the dawn. We are not separate; we are one, the lofty eagle, the majestic swan and the howling wolf that stands on the tundra hardened by ancient rock. It is my feeling, and my joy to know what a lucky boy I am to play my sweet refrain in the ark and concert of life.

MY PROFOUND LOVE FOR NATURE

I recall, in sweet nostalgia, my initiation into the wonder and beauty of nature. As a small child, transfixed by some Sweet Williams and meditating on the ethereal flight of a ghost moth, I fell in love. It is the colour, complexity and harmony of the many species that I find fascinating. To be outside in a cool breeze with ever-changing cloud patterns can be bliss. I can sit, with eyes closed in an oak wood, and identify each bird from the orchestra of nature, and the thrill song of a canary makes my eardrums vibrate.

Many days of youth, before I joined the madding crowd of London, found me alone with nature in the Wash wilderness. Since those days I have come alive in the mountains of the Himalaya, the swirling heat in mirages of deserts and salt lakes, and in fertile seas - a baptism into the wonders of the earth. A single structure of the hand of man looms large - the Golden Temple of Amritsar. In some respects, man is a blot on the landscape.

FIREFLY

I want to be a firefly to light up and fill the sky with burning magic, to rise up and burst with beauty, radiate and sparkle in the heavens. It will be a glorious fusion of raw creative power, transcendent in each waking hour. I will glow and shine like a fiery diamond, in shimmering moments of pure awe. In a glittering metamorphosis, my destiny will be sealed, a vision of pure fantasy.

DAYS THAT CHANGED MY LIFE

Head in the clouds in blissful absorption, I was captivated by the colourful acrobats of the warm summer sky. These were the birds of a young man's dream fulfilment, my Birmingham roller pigeons. Spinning and rolling and creating beautiful speed sensations, I became transfixed; my little world was complete. The aerial performance dance of these exotic birds is a true wonder and a mystery of the avian world. An aesthete's delight, a truly lovely spectacle, they inspire the deepest contemplation, approaching transcendence. In the depths of the countryside, summer after summer, I enjoyed the joyous detachment of these little bundles of athleticism.

NATURE AND ME

People study and write about conservation and nature, which is encouraging. The essence of being on earth, I feel, is a profound sense and deep experience of belonging to it, for we do not own the earth - we belong to it. I was first captivated by a ghost moth in the 50s, and some Sweet William flowers which resonated below the conscious intellect. Since those days of formative sense and sensibility, I have luxuriated in the oceans, mountains, deserts and forests of the world, and come to awareness on the edge of danger and on the pulse of life in wilderness, the whispering sands of the Sahara and the lofty world of eagles, free spirits that soared on high thermals in the Himalaya. An impact with the elements that give life to other beings is both transcendent and spiritually awakening, since man is pure spirit in a worldly and physical husk, which will return to Earth on the completion of its brief moment in time.

A BASIC LOVE FOR NATURE

To be out in the wilds of the world, in the mountains, deserts and seas has been a true epiphany for me. I have found the sights and sounds of the living world inspire wonder at their sheer spectacle and beauty. I give scant regard to inanimate objects, as they are soulless and will never light with fire and life. I have walked out often into the driving wind and rain and felt the snowflakes cling to my face. You come alive in remote wilderness and on the edge of survival, instincts honed from deep within a brain that is electrified. The whole essence and belief is that you are a little soul in the great web of vibrant life on earth and far from the madding crowd of city torment. It is a place where men may become giants of the spirit in the vastness of life.

A MYRIAD SEEDLINGS

My border is going to be a botanist's dream, with a plethora of wild flowers, nasturtiums, sweet peas, summer bulbs, gladioli, herbaceous plants and climbers. It is original and will be called the Emerton Impression Border, requiring a flora for indent purposes. Lacking the formality and predictability of formal bedding, it is based on niche survival of individual species in a specific location. As a contemplative poet, I study and probe life forms every day. My tubs on the gravel are glowing with mixed spring bulbs, to be chased along by toadflax and assorted native species. With so many genera I will concentrate on beauty rather than nomenclature. I studied nature as a child, eventually graduating in ecology and conservation in rural studies teaching. I retain a great love of the non-material and spiritual life.

THE BOY'S ADVENTURE TALE

When I was young there was so much fun to be had in the woods by the lake hunting high and low for the fox and the deer. My world was strange and insular, in mountains, forests and peninsula, as each pulse of freedom was born on the wings of adventure. At one with the outside world, every nuance unfurled in a time of make-believe. What wonders to perceive, in the song thrush, finch and grebe. The inviting, perfect nest was a wonderfest, a lasting image of a youth well spent in the timeless memories of yesterday when I was young, in pure naïve innocence.

THE HOUSEBOAT

In the wild, remote sea washes she faced the salt-laden winds, fresh with a tinge of iodine from the North Sea. It was a young man's dream to slip under the army blankets on the bunk and plan the next wildfowling foray into the saltings and the stalk edges. Silent contemplation and a soaring imagination were punctuated by the singular and rugged presence of the Wild Goose Man of the Wash, Kenzie Thorpe. What wild adventures we pursued in icebound sunsets, in swirling winds borne of snowflakes that clung to our beards and melted with the rush of warm air from our nostrils. The Tilly lamp flickered as hard case eccentrics exchanged colourful stories, fuelled by beans, soup and eggs rendered edible on a smoky paraffin stove.

As the moon cast her melancholy light over the seascape, plaintive cries of curlew haunted the dank air, grey seals surfaced and little terns, so graceful and magical, dived into the icy waters below. The elements exhilarated us and the spirit soared, leaving traces of wonder in an old man's reflections.

DECEMBER IN MY GARDEN

Many genera of bulbs are up including narcissi, crocus and galanthus. The poppy seedlings and wildflower species are having a go. I trust in nature and believe all will balance out in the wondrous cycle that is beyond the comprehension of mere man. It was great to see dipterous flies pollinating the Fatsia japonica well into the month. In true symbolism a robin sang from a maple in the driving rain, with sanguine resilience. I meditate in my enclave on a daily basis, as a source of Zen and inspiration to my work.

WHERE THE WILD WIND BLOWS

Where the wild wind blows, deep in the remote Wash wilderness and swept off my feet by a howling gale, I slithered down the grassy bank of the sea wall, halted only by a lonely dyke and a potato field. On into the murk, and in the looming night I pulled out two mallard with a single report from my trusty twelve bore. Floating on a tidal creek, the two prize specimens were just retrievable.

Time to take the lonely walk back to my womb of civilisation, the lonely spectre of Kenzie Thorpe's houseboat, moored way back on the saltings. Alone and free in this rugged and testing landscape, I was intoxicated by the grandeur of my very own boy's adventure tale. In the vibrant and setting sun, awesome streams of wild geese skeins orchestrated the evening sky, as the soft murmurings of pinkfoot geese introduced an eerie, rich silence. Life on the houseboat, with its raw and rugged simplicity, created a state of intense mindfulness, aroused by deep and primitive survival instincts - a young man alone in a land where the wild wind blows.

ZEN

Summer breeze drifting and floating, light as a feather, in the essence of my mind. Free as a foaming waterfall, bubbling from the whirlpool within, as my spirit transcends the cares of men, in pure feelings of Zen. Cool as an ice crystal on the sea of life, kissed by warm and gentle rays, these are my finest days at one with beautiful things - it is the way.

II

THE HUMAN CONDITION

HUMAN KINDNESS

Now that you're famous, rich and clever

Money lasting for evermore

Just take time to reflect

And make sure you connect

From the annals of your mind

See what you can find

Listen to the voice of reason

Find a little understanding

Because human kindness is overflowing

And I think it's going to rain today.

EVE OF DESTRUCTION

The world is going plastic

Consuming Earth quite drastic

The forests are polluted

Since everyone commuted

People have expanded

With ever more demanded

The human race has wasted

All the Earth's wealth tasted

Soon God's only creation

The end of all the nation

As we suffer endless fright

The start of Arctic night

The end of the world is nigh

As a meteor falls from the sky.

THE INTROVERT

My life is in my head
Not in what you just said
My feelings are remote
Detached, I do not vote
I am singular, quirky and peculiar
Unworldly and detached
My rich imagination has just hatched
A smashing set of new ideas
To satisfy my own desires.

THE EXTROVERT

Being famous, rich and flash,
Sure to cut a racy dash
Amusing, funny, a smarty,
Star of the very best party
My sports car shines bright red
I'm willing to jump into bed
The mainstream holds me dear
Of others I have no fear
I am one of the army
My blazer made by Armani
Who is the oddball subvert?
Must be an introvert
Showing my very best bling
Always up for a fling.

THE WINNER

Reflection, the silver dream spelling my name out loud

Today I am so proud

Standing on top of a mountain so high

A lofty beacon in the sky

I am the spirit of number one

Competitors all have been outshone

In celestial heavens I shine so high

Sprinkling stardust for you and I

I am the greatest living soul

The rest have had to pay the toll

I am immortal, a massive high on your very own living icon.

GOSSIP

The community I live in is very forgiving

As it vibrates to the tune of chattering human voices

Spirits lonely, feeling now at one

With the local collective

As the summer air echoes to the sound of eager souls

Like a host of sparrows

Adding tone and colour to local music

Exploring identities

Exchanging emotions in excited and urgent self-expression

The Earth absorbing each shallow sound into the core of its being.

KNOW-ALL OR SAGE?

A scientist, a polyglot

Thinks he knows the lot

An icon of society

Of fame, riches, notoriety

Yet in the great cosmic scheme
Does he not see his own human reflection
In each conscious question?
The long search for the absolute truth
Is not tainted by the human condition itself
In the reduction to nothing.
So what is ultimate reality?
Perhaps Santa is the sage.

MENSA

We all get into the queue
To test our brilliant IQ
We are mental paragons of genius
Mind and arrogance
We really think we've cracked it
Our little card of plastic
Whilst pondering in our digs
We sit and write some SIGS
In all we seek and find
The beauty of our mind.

ALIENATION

Falling, spiralling down into an empty void
Feeling the chill of despair
 Consumed by a world of nothingness
Mind broken by the flame of insanity
No hope, no faith, no feelings
Staring at the empty ceiling.
The Saviour will not come for me
Gripped by the vice of paranoia.

ARMAGEDDON

The good, the evil, the minds of men on earthly soil

Emerging from collective man

Jousting in a primordial attempt to rule

It is the nature of man since notions of Adam and Eve were conceived

The very first speak

The primal footprint in the book of history

Individual man may unite this human duality

So that the sage may be born from out of psychic chaos.

DEATH

In the darkest shadows of the psyche

Lurks the ultimate reality of man

Power so absolute, so total without escape

Waiting to take us to eternity

To the void, to the centre of its core

And when our Earthly quest is done

Our dust and atoms will make it whole

From the moment of our birth

Death has us in its mighty grip

SILVER TROPHY

The human dream

The name reflected on the symbol of solid silver

It is the fame impulse

A searing need for others' recognition that we are alive

We are human, we are unique

Yet part of a thrusting mass of psychic energy.

Silver trophy with immortality twinkling from its reflective eye

The Western urge to cement an ego within an earthly lifetime.

WAR

We send young men to maim and destroy
Objects of all political ploy
Everywhere around the world
Male egos still abound
The process just goes on and on
Blood-soaked fields under earthly sun
Why do men engage with utility
In stupid acts of grave futility?
Never will man know the prize
Of peace, love and need to be wise.

THE MYSTIC MAN

The mystic man, his spirit brim full of truth
Has pierced the deceptions of conscious reason
Penetrated the secrets of human existence
And found himself united with the whole
With wisdom profound and self-secured
He takes his eternal place within the bosom
Of the cosmic sphere
Strange to the West and maligned by something
He tastes the sweet nectar of life's experience.

OUTER BODY EXPERIENCE

Two bodies united as one
Bombarding each other with pure ecstasy
The rapture, the liberation of spirits
United in space, in time
In the free air of sexual unity
Outside the norm
An existential form.

ANTIPODEAN NATIVE

This beautiful land, full of magic of earthly spirits

Gave rise to me, and I belong to it

I am the Earth, and she is me, we are one

My spirit rises with the morning sun

Rests and sleeps at its setting

I see the starlit sky

It is the roof of my being

My body will feed and succour life.

MIND AND BODY

To avoid any confusion

They are both one and fusion

Mind and brain are centre of the husk

The engine at the heart of us

Body then to all mankind

A physical statement of the mind

It can be very dramatic

To be ill and psychosomatic

The body is a temple

Physical and fundamental.

SURVIVOR

A man must face his destiny on the rocky road of life. He is an island washed by the cruel and turbulent sea of humanity. Living on the edge of the abyss, you may stare the prospect of death in the face. Your consciousness may ignite primal instincts from the base of the brain. I took a trip into this zone in Afghanistan, where the light hit my naive eyes and I felt a surge of reality. With good fortune a good life may leave a footprint in the sands of time, a reminder that a little life was spent on Planet Earth. Success is not the things that you have from a life of toil, it is who you are. Some may feel a spiritual glow from deep within, and this gentle epiphany is the way to truth.

KNOCKING AT THE DOOR OF DEATH

Life on the edge alerts the senses, activates the spirit and makes you come alive. I do what I can, having survived Afghanistan, the insane heat of India and the baptism of serious travel. Now my passport is not in the eye of the wind, as the sun glistens on the Sahara, but in the eye of my mind. The liberty of consciousness is the freedom of the soul, not an alien, a singular whole. In salt-laden winds, a bright golden sun, I shone with light and was born again. I did not fight the stars at night and surrendered myself to the infinite cosmos. The lifespan of man is not the possession you hold in the palm of your hand but an ear that hears the bird that calls, the warm summer breeze on butterfly wings and all the beautiful things I have felt, seen and done.

SPIRIT HIGH

Raise me up right to the clouds, let me float in a sea of beauty.

Beyond the spade, the earth and clod, I need to fly in the face of God.

A gentle stirring of the wind lifts me like an autumn leaf, to fall as light as gossamer to the open arms of Mother Earth.

Material man does not know of the ethereal glow that I love to know with each single breath I take. Euphoria is what I feel, an escape from physical constraints in the normality I forsake.

My mission is a journey of truth, a lonely voice in the big wide world, where I make sense of the strange and the absurd.

A TEARDROP EXPLODES

If I could cry, I would fill the world with tears. My brain is a well of emotion that overflows as the teardrop explodes.

The troubles I have seen, the struggle, anguish and pain will always remain, as a single drop falls gently from cheek. The feeling soul of mankind can fill oceans, lakes and seas in sweet catharsis.

Tears are the conduit that liberates and frees us like a paradise bird that dances in ecstasy. Why be a prisoner of the conscious mind, when you can set the spirit free?

THE RECLUSE

Behind the door, the screen, the hedge, a little man lives out his lonely dream. I would love to pierce his outer shell, to see the being deep within, as he emerges from the tomb of withdrawal from a cruel, harsh world.

A wondrous spirit, a creative genius may have sought refuge in the inner world that he seeks to escape from the men at large, the everyday freaks. This man failed to come alive, in the daily grind of the nine till five. He found a spirit deep within, that was the well of his power and beauty. Who am I to disagree with the life he forsakes and the steps that he takes to set the spirit free?

THE PERSONALITY MASK

With time and age, I aim to be as exactly as I am with others. Many people conceal their inner selves or true natures behind ego morphs or masks, as I have done myself. Who are these people, I ask? A perceptive/intuitive I can be used to discern a true perception of them. Sophisticated people on the stage of society may take some probing.

The great authors like Kafka, Dostoevsky and Blake fascinated me as I tried to penetrate their minds. Carl Jung went very deep in his many volumes, as did Sartre. It is certain that we do not get to the hardcore of inner reality of other people. In my travels I have seen them on the edge of survival, primal and instinctive, where the drive to maintain integrity and life are the limiting factors. I do like to pierce the shallow veneer of human relationships. Can you see the real me - can you?

ILLUSION AND DELUSION

In my time on Earth, with frequent travel around the world, I have analysed many personality traits in people. It fascinates me to consider what many believe to be reality or the true nature of earthly experience. There is a great deal of myth, convention and prejudice expressed in print and daily chat. I try and sift through it all for some intrinsic truth. Many people take on the influences and propaganda in the media, whereas a more detached, cautious approach may illuminate the facts.

In my life I have met some people, or read about them, who have great individual integrity and character. I am drawn to creative people and innovators in their field, and have learned many things from them. With their charisma and esoteric knowledge, they become magnetic people. Just probe and discern what you hear and see, and perceive how much smacks of reality.

SEA OF SOULS

The oceans of humanity are seas of lost souls that float on the surfaces of shallow currents. They are remnants of the mainstream, brainwashed by the media, rules and conventions. A man must stand alone and face the depths of himself to be real and true; only then can he be singular and free. New waves of creativity and hope are made by those with an inner voice who bang the drum and fly the flag of hope and inspiration. The cultures in historical time bear witness to the brave souls who have probed the fathoms as they dive towards the abyss.

OVERCONFIDENCE AND DELUSION

In the blindness of youthful arrogance and optimism, we can con ourselves into pretending that we are superior and know it all. These false notions are perpetuated by a rampant ego, often male. Now, with the power of reflective insight and wisdom, there is little that we know in an absolute sense, since total understanding of anything escapes man. When you open your mind and strip it down to basal instincts you may have glimpses of the truth or essence of things on a personal level, which adds to your philosophy. Expertise in specialist subjects leads to status and credibility in society, and the word 'genius' has become very common in popular consciousness as we like to judge other people. Fundamental to humanity is the need to establish an identity.

ELITISM AND CLASS CONSCIOUSNESS

In a fame-driven society, led by hungry egos, people seek recognition to bolster their self-esteem. It is found in celebrity culture, elitist and specialist groups, hierarchies, fanaticisms, and is the nucleus of popular culture. Perceptions of personal identity in relation to class and feelings of ethnicity and race are rampant traits in the collective psyche. They are underpinned by the competitive spirit for self-realisation and individuality. In my perceptional innovations, creative changes and fresh insights are made by singular specialists, or elitists who manifest a richness and diversity of talents. Popularity is often based on charisma, which may be tangible to the sensitive eye. I believe there is an obvious inequality and class consciousness in many cultures based on an understanding of elitism.

PERSONALITY

As a quiet, introverted boy I was flushed by the idea of being and personality. A rather egocentric notion, I set out in life to try and cultivate one. At 67 years old, and now in reflection, an interesting metamorphosis has taken place. My outer personality transmuted from scholar to gardener to teacher to sales/businessman. The changes have been suffused by a restless need for change and instability, yet I love the mature morph as poet, writer and philosopher. The future is one of consolidation until the physical form is recycled, and the inner man leaves a trace of words and memories.

THE COMPLAINTS CULTURE

I see it and hear it each and every day, the negative cynicism of criticism and the unloading of negative moods on to politics, people, events and every conceivable external influence. Pessimism equates to psychological failure, in my philosophy. People resent the power and control of governments, hierarchies, bosses and committees. The quintessence of happiness to me is freedom, space and positive self-expression in an acceptable medium. A degree of personal spirituality, when experienced by the inner man, may contribute to self-realisation of the individual person. 'Do your own thing' was a wise dictum of the psychedelic subculture. If you can find some peace and harmony in nature, then it is worth millions in dirty money. My piece is a little complaint, yet is so pertinent in Western capitalist society.

LOWDOWN BUM

Dark, depressed and down and out, alone, desperate without a shout, I clung on to an inner spark that would ignite the forgotten flame.

Who knows the destiny of each man - a single voice in a lifespan?

We are sailing ships that pass in the night, on the oceans of humanity.

With the passage of time, I look through the chapters of my life, and have been moved by the birds that fly, the wasps that sting, the wonderful and beautiful things; the jewels of nature that have touched me to the core.

One day when the sun goes down, the stars will shine on my illustrious life.

ALONE AM I

The people of the world, the teeming masses of humanity, are individual spirits, that interconnect in a giant social organism. I enjoy some communication with others, yet always revert to base, aware of my singularity of being in an existential sense. I have encountered many lost souls in my life who lacked a real perception of their own core identity. These folk are in need of a comforting inner spirituality. I found mine in wild and remote places of the world, at risk, and on the edge of survival in Afghanistan. To a man of sensibility life has more to offer than shallow materialism, yet who are we behind the mask in the human theatre of life?

SPIRITS, GODS AND DEVILS

In the culture of humanity since primordial man, there are traces or traits common to beliefs, art, thought, literature and other outward manifestations of the brain/mind synthesis. These engrams, or recurring phenomena, were well documented by Carl Gustav Jung, whose penetrating insight into himself and others was profound. I believe that the collective psyche of man in response to and in synchrony with an external world has created the phantoms, myths, legends and other powerful effects of the human condition. On an existential level, and in the inner and spiritual elements of the perceived self they have significance and may be demonstrated as art, religion, sanity and madness, where significance will depend on the social mores of the time. All these entities are common to people, and perhaps exist beyond the earthly sphere in the vastness of the cosmos.

IMAGE

In society people present their outward personalities in a certain way, to make a response, impact or impression. There are many actors out there, yet some people behave in a genuine way, and can be said to be honest. A sharp, discerning and perceptive mind can spot who is who in the theatre of life. When all the ego morphs and games run out, who are we? It is a true sage who knows himself!

In everyday social exchanges, I like to flow along and take the easiest route with others -social and emotional harmony are important. People play roles, eg teacher or actor, when masks may well be donned. Some smart tricks are pulled by conmen, and they are common. It is fascinating to suss out who is who in the sea of social experiences of the images that we create and cultivate.

THE FIRE OF MY IMAGINATION

In the cauldron of my mind, a furnace I can find. The brain is a serpent of fire that fuels my desire, in words of heat and passion that flow from deep within.

The dreams of a man are the emblems of a truth that only he can know. I like to go beyond the norm, a bird's eye view at the heart of a storm. To feel the rain fall down my cheeks, a sense of earth upon my feet, as I hear the birds within the woods, the pulse of nature is understood. A man must walk alone and call the flame his very own, before the candle snuffs right out.

PRESSING THE EDGE OF REASON

Some aspects of human experience, of the psyche and consciousness, stretch the boundaries of rational explanation. What is in the minds of people described as mad or genius? We may think we have a perception of this type of experience, yet different cultures in the human world describe these variants in different ways, celebrating them in art, music, literature and the popular consciousness of the times. My belief is that the innermost depth of each person makes them truly enigmatic. When we attempt to examine individuals using verbal language, we see a shallow ripple on the sea of man. This idea can be illustrated by attempts to know the nature of iconic figures like Einstein, Picasso, or da Vinci, as well as everyman. I think the great questions facing humankind are beyond absolute understanding, due to our limited little minds. A search for omniscience may lead to delusion.

LESSONS I HAVE LEARNED IN LIFE

With experience in wilderness, rugged and remote Afghanistan, and into the Himalaya, I have learned many things. It is a wise man who knows himself, and who can recognise friend and foe for who they are. When the instinct for survival kicks in, you are on your own with your own resources as an individual being. When the chips are down, social groups tend to fragment into single people with their egos.

This is my perception of humanity, having been amongst teeming masses of them throughout the world. If you can realise your dreams and continue a dream, then some lasting contentment may be the consequence. It is not only the life that you have led, but the legacy you leave as a trace of who you are. Life is about personal identity and the codes and standards that you set in your time on Planet Earth.

DICING WITH DEATH

Like the lesson of the moth, you can tempt the core of the candle flame, and risk being burned by beauty. In my brief sojourn on Planet Earth, I have walked the tightrope of possibility. A man may crave the intoxication of the fireblade of experience, or hide behind the cushion of a comfortable life. Too much exposure in the fast lane will leave its scars, as a ticket is the price you may pay for euphoria. With time and age, you may reflect with sweet nostalgia on the heady excesses of youth, when craving and desire were king, and you held the world in the palm of your hand. If you live hard enough and long enough, a nebulous past may be clarified by insight - the truth.

OUT-OF-BODY EXPERIENCES

These are not that unusual in people as a whole. I have had two such experiences in my colourful and exciting past. Common to both was a strong and pure feeling of the inner spirit as a powerful entity, as a being and presence in free air outside the physical body. The memories evoked were vivid and personality changing. There are popular explanations for these in psychological/scientific and spiritual terms. I am happy with the reality of my own inner experiences, which are pleasant in nostalgic recall - one at Stirling University and the other in Kashmir. They were both ecstatic in intensity.

PRESSING THE EDGE OF REASON

Some aspects of human experience, of the psyche and consciousness, stretch the boundaries of rational explanation. What is in the minds of people described as madmen or geniuses? We may think we have a perception of this type of experience, yet different cultures in the human world describe these variants in different ways, celebrating them in art, music, literature and the popular consciousness of the times. My belief is that the innermost depth of each person makes them truly enigmatic. When we attempt to examine individuals using verbal language, we see a shallow ripple on the sea of man. This idea can be illustrated by attempts to know the nature of iconic figures like Einstein, Picasso or da Vinci, as well as everyman. I think the great questions facing humankind are beyond absolute understanding, due to our limited little minds. The search for omniscience may lead to delusion.

THE RISE OF THE MACHINE

When machines were mice and men were lions, we did not think of the times when technology would rule the minds of men as inanimate gods. Men need to tune into the calls from the soul and the echoes of instincts deep within. In the deep-seated schism that divides men from their true nature, the computer becomes a revered object of love and devotion, alongside the shallow face of texting and endless uttering of shallow consequence. Oh for a love of all that is wild and free with a little spirituality! Then we may see a little sensitivity, love and harmony in response to the rise of the machine.

III

THE STUDY OF MANKIND

THE POLITICIAN

I am a quasi-intellectual
Effete and ineffectual
To consort with spies, and spin you lies
I will use up all expenses
Never join the Mensas
With the craft of a cat
To con you with chat.
I will beguile you with my charm
Trick you and make you disarm
I am a master of the spiel
That slips like an eel
With every promise I made
I left you all in the shade
Some think I'm It, to leave you in the sh*t.

TALENT

Let exquisite form stand above the norm
Sing your song, write more words
Bring joy to the hearts of men
Serve them with a fountain pen
Feel the rapture, taste the applause
You are the one, you are the cause
Now you've made it you are a star
A shining light from near and far.

THE TRICKSTER

The trickster lures with easy charm
Motives you to well disarm
With poise and grace he takes his place

Object - to con the human race.
With dazzling smile and warmth of feeling
He aims to hit a lofty ceiling
To break your heart and leave you broke
He'll fund another line of coke
Exactly knowing words to utter
Well and truly in the gutter.

PCSO

I'm the local PCSO
In the community so here we go,
Approaching every thief and crook
Never let them off the hook
I patrol the streets and alleyways
In search of bad men and affrays
Always staying honest and true
Helping people in a stew
Riding around on my little bike
Protecting the Yorkie and the tyke
I will uphold the spirit of the law
Knocking on each single door.

FREDDIE

He was a little Russell
Born for hustle and bustle
Really warmed my heart
From the very start
I used to tell him stories
Of rabbits, rats and forays
He could tell what you were thinking

Instincts shared and distinctive
I won't forget this little dog
A blessing from Our Lord the God
I will always see him at the gate
A lovely chap, my very best mate.

MONEY

Some make a God of a little note
Spend their lives in pursuit of wealth
When all that counts is just their health
Material things loom large and clear
Anything else a little queer
Life has more to offer than this
The rat race just creates a tiz
Richness of mind is more the prize
Reducing money down to size

THE ARTIST

I bring you beauty above the norm
Paint a picture, the eye of the storm
Inform you, transform you, a feast for the senses
I am one of the very best Mensas
My words paint a colourful picture
Of metaphor, simile and scripture
I light a fire in imagination's eye
With you until the day you die

THE COMEDIAN

With wit and perspicacity
I raise the roof with hilarity

My humour is infectious
Adapted well and dextrous
The audience can't resist it
To belly laugh, I insist it
Now I'm rich and famous
The whole world will proclaim us.

MISTER COOL

I am no fool, the epitome of cool
Staying so calm when others have balm
Excitement of human race
Leaves me right off the pace
When the situation gets dicey
I switch off and get icy.
In all the commotion
I have no emotion
When others go forward
I remain horizontal
The top they go over
I nearly fall over
At parties they stayed back
While I remained laid back
The ladies just drool
Cos I'm Mister Cool.

HENDRIX

He was a force of nature
Far out, and way out of sight
Purple haze was in his brain
As he just kissed the sky
High on cocaine, a man never mundane
Brought his gifts with every riff

His genius just amazed
The memory never fades
A God with sounds sublime
Music beyond his time
He played louder and so much faster
The master of the Stratocaster.

FAME

They believe they know me in the outer world
Reading of me, talking about me
An entity, mere object of illusions, of discussions
Yet I am private, in the darkness and behind the shadows.
Fame cannot know the unknowable
We walk through life a seething mass of islands.

JANUS FACE

Can you see the real me, can you?
What games we humans play
The tricks of the ego, the acts we portray
Many deceits to conceal the self
Conforming to outer needs, needs of the world
When we find the truth we stand alone
A rock bold, hard and strong
In the foaming sea of humanity
A whole person, a singular identity.

THE ECCENTRIC

Free from constraints and tethers
The eccentric beats a singular pulse
Sweet music orchestrated by himself
In the tiresome mass of conformity

He stands alone
Yet new waves, new sounds from the worldly drum
Generate loud from his lone voice
In time society may embrace him as the norm
Hooray for Lady Gaga
Shine on you crazy diamond!
Glitter for the world to see.

THE FISHERMAN

Sitting by the silver stream
I ponder, think and dream
Of what wonders lurk below
The silken weed, the ebb, the flow
A dragonfly cuts across the sky
Magic to my human eye
Will I catch a pike today
To reward me for my long stay?
After hours and hours
I sense the powers
I'm in the wake
Of this mighty lake.

SHALLOW FM

Tuning in to the waves
The sounds that I crave
Of sweet music
Yet I am so critical
Nothing yet mystical
About the fast-flowing
Never knowing, utterly cynical
Verbal nonsense

From the ever so cool
And utter fool
Ego he craves
The dominant airwaves
On the crest of his career
Splash of verbal diarrhoea
I have to condemn
Tuning to shallow FM.

THE USER

Behind my cunning charm
Your naive trust I disarm
You fall for my guile
Result of my smile
As I kid you, con you, outsmart you
I am the abuser, soothsayer and user
Here to stay
In the cold light of day.
One day you may get quizzical
Thoughtful, philosophical
And aim to be my mimic
A wizened, gnarled old cynic.

MR STEALTHY

Quiet as a ghost
I make the most of my artful charm
Your very soul to disarm
Meek and mild, I go with guile
To the sweet core of your being
Where my ego sows seeds
The forests of the future

You think I'm kind in the essence of your mind
I am the calculator, the Shaolin monk
Plotting my young scheme
Is the nature of my dream.
There is so much clout
In the whisper, louder than the shout.

FOR GILBERT

He is a grand old boy
Pigeons are his game
They bring him joy and fame
From Croydon he descends
A man without pretence
It was his youthful dream
On high, to glide across the sky
From aircraft high he leapt
A spirit away was swept
His daring knew no bounds
No parachute was found.
With lofty spirit, self-possessed
And gay abandon, never wept
As he flew through life
With the taste of sweet freedom.

THE SAVANT

My genius courses through my single and remote world
Each vibration of sound tingles my sensations
The music I hear floods my soul with beauty
My spirit soars along each violin note
You gaze upon my being with ignorance and curiosity
Absorbed as I unite myself with the instrument of spheres
In notes of the gods.

MIRROR MAN

Mirror, mirror on the wall

Who has the grandest ego of them all?

With self-centred magnificence

Vanity, absorption and grandiloquence

He stares at the beautiful Narcissus

An image of the gods, from beyond the stars

Sun-toned skin highlighting a face of pure symmetry

Eyes, fiery pools of human beauty

Reflecting a soul perfected

By human poetry

I am the greatest human hero

The grand delusion of my ego.

THE EGO

I am a florid narcissus

Magnificent, always with us

The master of delusion

Never forced into seclusion

I fly on the wings of fame

Brazen, bold and with no shame

I know that I will go far

A celestial being, a superstar

In all weathers, stormy and foul

It's me, the wondrous Simon Cowell

THE BULLSHITMAN

To spin you a yarn

Is part of my charm

Let's create a little fantasy

My craft and guile for all to see.
My words are like a sleuth
You think I tell the truth
Yet I con you, disarm you
Beguile you and smarm you
Master of wit, a huge hitter
To you, a great big bullshitter

THE TRAMP

Far from the throng
I sing my song of sweet freedom
Walking every highway
Hedgerow, field and byway
The lines on my brow
The here and the now
Tell of my human storm
Days of dark shadows
Demons and hallows
Yet in the setting sun
I see so much fun
To live at my pace
No more the rat race
The sea, the sun, the stars
Magic behind closed doors.

THE POSEUR

Florid exterior firing the stage
Metaphor, simile on every page
The narcissus is in full bloom
To make sexy ladies swoon

With ego fit to burst
Shallow interior cursed
Libidinous, blithe and randy
He is a showcase dandy
In clothes styled by Armani
We think him a bit barmy.

THE CROONER

My easy charm caresses the stage
Velvet voice from the musical page
I kiss the senses
Seduce the defences
My voice is of beautiful rapture
Heart and soul I will capture
I sing my song, my star shines bright
The pulsating throng know it's just right.

ROCK STAR

Each sexy strut of my outrageous ego
Guitar tuned in to my libido
The cadence of my voice, a sexy instrument of fine choice
I am an image of girly dreams
Of untold fantasy, and lovers' schemes
Lighting up the stage a force of creation
Superstar of all our nations
A cultural icon in full flow
My gifts on you I will bestow
Better than Clapton, Plant and Hendrix
Others I make a mere appendix
From another planet, I am so cosmic

To bring you shivers and thrills orgasmic
On the lips of each soothsayer
The very answer to your prayer.

THE MENTOR

I make them laugh and make them cry
As the birds they learn to fly
They search for knowledge, seek the truth
I am the wizard, the wise, the sleuth
to rule the roost, give them boost
Their future destiny is in my hands
Teaching minds that they will understand
That to be famous is the mainstream dream
A product of the mentor's scheme
To search their soul is my worldly role
Travelling space and time will make them whole.

THE CHAV

With my monosyllabic grunt
I will give you a right good shunt
My head is bright and so shiny
My brain is small and tiny
If we ever meet, I'll kick you off the street
From one council house to another
I am the lord of my manor
Carrying crowbar, bat and spanner
Going far to hot-wire your car
My name is Wayne, your very own star.

THE EVIL GENIUS

With his magnificent conception
To fool the world with deception
With malevolent intent, he is hell bent
He aims to rule the world
His satanic ego unfurled
To control, power and destroy you
Mere objects of paranoia
With charisma and force of oratory
He fuels his ethnic laboratory
A paranoid schizophrenic
Expert on eugenics.

SCHIZOID MAN

When society will ask
He dons a mask
To protect the inner man
From a worldly scan
In a veil of fear
Feelings unclear
The inner man is all embracing
Persona self-effacing
Often not sentimental
Calculating, cool and elemental
His vision is lofty and creative
The liberation from the scream
Of alienation
As he struggles not to be consumed
The empty cell of schizoid man.

PRETTY THINGS

I love pretty things
Jewels that sparkle and diamond rings
When my spirit starts to drop
I go for a jolly good shop
Dress up in my glad rags
Buying blouses, shoes and handbags
I shop as hard as I can
In search of another bargain.
We love the cosy simplicity
Of little chats and cups of tea
A primal urge for the new
A really girly thing to do.

THE SURREALIST

The artist, a cauldron of the unconscious
Projects imagery into the light of consciousness
Seducing us, transfixing us
With unearthly wonders
To feed our hungry senses
Satisfy eager minds.
One day the *avant garde*
Will transmute into popular culture
Everyday man will be lured into the temple of the aesthetic.

VAN GOGH

Each stroke of florid brilliance
An outpouring from the inferno
The need to purify, cleanse a troubled soul
And when the genius is projected

The retreat into the inner chamber of torment
The sunflowers only partly satisfy
The need to set the spirit free
Escape from the tortured vice of inner man
We sense him now
Immortalised in beauty.

AQABA

The craggy herdsman seated alone
Beckoned me to join him there
Sharing the cool water from a silver jug
Offering chicken split fresh from the sizzling bird
Sharing moments of rare connection;
Yet not a word is spoken
The note he gave me bore his name
A proud, benign Arab herdsman.

THE MONK

A shaolin priest with mind of steel
Goes beyond what we can feel
With grace and poise he takes his place
Way beyond the human race.
He knows himself, he has no doubts
The master of the sword and flail
His body forged completes the tale.

THE PSYCHIC

The psychic sees beyond the normal
Making sense of fleeting moments of possibilities
Bringing reality to the nebulous and the vague

Clearing a path into the future
Eyes illumined, he pierces the shadows
And shines a torch of truth and of reality
His voice is heard by those who know.

THE OPIUM EATER

There was a man in Afghanistan
Who took the black tar of euphoria
Bought in Chicken Street
Almost took his heartbeat
Withdrawing into the husk
The ashen face a physical bust.
American travellers examined the shell
They dared not tell of narcotic hell
But from the depths of early grave
A spirit rose, a life to crave!

BEAUTY QUEEN

Gracious, elegant, serene
The world's finest beauty queen
Flowing across the floor
She loves to be adored
A painted lady, so ethereal
Visionary beyond the material
Her fame secured and sound
Our senses are spellbound.

SEX

Let me come clean,
I'm just a sex machine
I use my charms, I drive them wild

Names in diaries are now filed
I rise and rise, create a boom
The ladies fall and swoon and swoon
My physical conquests are just fabulous
Lovers think I'm bold and amorous
I am famous, powerful and thin
The second coming of Errol Flynn.

THE INTELLECTUAL

Full of abstract thought, my feelings count for nought
I am the thinker, not a playboy or a drinker
I will inspect it, analyse it
Research it, dissect it and probe it
My books and articles are fabulous
Yet misunderstood and nebulous
Finally I must learn to be real
To take stock and know how to feel.

MR GRUMPY

I am old, fat and frumpy
They call me Mr Grumpy
I never get satisfaction
From my thoughts and their abstraction
My mood is often dark
Bare of joy and stark
I am full of negativity
Sour-faced, crabby and passivity
My need to make you miserable
Is heavy, great, considerable
Always keen and snappy
No wish to make you happy.

THE LUCID PROFESSOR

I am the master of intuition
Abstracts, concepts and cognition
My papers pass the censors
Prometheus, Giga and of Mensas
I lecture on global trips
With lofty manuscripts
An oddball in a team of us
The unworldly higher genius.

THE NEUROTIC

I am nervous, sensitive, vulnerable
Obsessive, odd and culpable
Lying in my bed, all the tears I shed
The tortured life I've led
Always feeling ill
Reaching for the pill
People make me so unhappy
Aggressive, awful and snappy
My boss is so despotic
To me he is an old neurotic.

DESPOT

With fear, delusion and loathing
The crazy ruler is foaming
At the mouth of humanity
With ruthless conviction and clarity
The masses will simply bow down
To this, the supremo clown
His power is insistent

To quell the mind of dissidents.
One day the people will rise up
To make room for another
Pretender to the throne of illusion.

MIDDLE-CLASS AFFECTATIONS

Hi Caroline, how's the foie gras?
Is your son a superstar?
The Jag is ever so charming
Oiks are so alarming
Wearing my tweeds from Harris
The Old Masters in Paris
I love to hear the Chopin
Watch Monet, Degas and Gauguin
Then we'll meet at Betty's
Wedding frothed with confetti
We dwell in lofty, grand houses
Our egos inflated, as our spouses
The proletariat are lower and denser
Our IQs are fit for MENSA.

THE CALL GIRL

The soft, seductive red light
Alerts my senses to primal possibilities
Urged on by lustful instincts
I knock at the dark door of love
A sultry nymph lures me to her web of illicit love
Fired by passion's heat
We indulge in the ancient transaction
The merging of human needs
In glorious acts of primordial satisfaction.

THE DWARF

I am the little dwarf
I wish I could grow and morph
Very small and insignificant
My ego bold, magnificent
In my imagination
I am the world of fascination
Within my soul I am a lionheart
Leader of men right from the start
I tower above the world with finality
Impress them all, a personality.

THE OPTIMIST

My glass is full right over
Now I'm in the clover
I smile and radiate the gladness
Cured of all my sadness
I am beaming and so charming
Joyous and disarming
My life is so glamorous
Now I'm famous, rich and amorous
Everything just falls in place
An icon of the human race.

GAMBLER'S FALLACY

My name is Bert
And I'm really on a cert
The race is off, some may scoff
But I'm really going to win
I play all the tables

Expert on all stables
I lead a merry dance
Take on every chance
Confident, sure to far go
Although I'm hard as flint
And utterly broke and skint.

WHO IS JOHN WEBSTER?

John Webster is a master of deception
Full of emotional complexity
Chameleon-like intensity
He varies as the wind
The old rogue now has sinned
Just cannot be well trusted
His ego has been busted
The job is garden digger
Personality a living enigma.

THE DRIPPING TAP

The endless dripping tap
Drives me to distraction
In fantasy, abstraction
It burrows in my brain
The mother of all pain
It makes me so, so sad
Driven almost mad
Will I let it rule me?
The tap is trying to fool me
Others will just scoff
I think I'll turn it off.

ANGEL OF DEATH

I am a spiritual force
To claim you a matter of course
I dwell in ghostly shadows
To scare you through to the marrow
The he-goat sends me for you
To pulverise and gore you
You will not escape my thunder
Never a single blunder
In deepest folklore dwell
The heart of living hell.

THE CAPITALIST ILLUSION

I will alter your perception
Inflate prices with deception
The master of illusion
Conception and confusion.
I will trick you and use you
Nail you and diffuse you
You will purchase all my bargains
Handbags, shoes and nylons
So that you remember
To become a bigger spender
You will not taste my honey
Because I'm here to take your money
Just hear my heart sing
The sound of every cash register
KA-CHING!
KA-CHING!

THE HUNTER

Hard and ruthless, dim and cruel
I shoot the pheasant, it is my fuel
From dark recesses of the mind
I make the choice to be unkind
Talk about it all as 'game'
As expert shot I know the fame
Master of nature I think I am
Taking all a great big scam
Yet I will never know
The richness of life in all its flow.

NO. 1 STAR

It's me, the No. 1 star
My name is Lady Gaga
The world knows how I feel
Crazy, odd, so surreal
I create the sound and fuse it
With my lovely music
I am huge and stellar
Music's greatest seller
Once I was unseen
Now centre of mainstream
I'm concave, linear concentric
The world's most famous eccentric.

THE TATTY TART

Fantasy girl in diamonds and pearls, a flirty feline with seductive charms of sensual promise, she raises lust in every seductive toss of her golden hair. Every young man wants to please the seductress and the exotic tease. She haunts the shadows, the bright lights and red lights, of the pulsating heart of city sleaze. Her world is profane, opium, hashish and cocaine. In the sultry heat of youth and yesterday, I longed for a hot and passionate stay in the arms of afternoon delights.

IV

PHILOSOPHY

THE MEANING OF LIFE

I have travelled around the world, studied, meditated, examined belief systems and philosophical thought processes and have made a few insights as follows. Under the influence of the cosmos and the brain/mind synthesis humanity does not know the nature of the intrinsic reality of the cosmos. Science, philosophy, religion and other human processes are based within the individual and collective consciousness of man and within the limits of language and consciousness. In the vastness of the cosmic space-time continuum, a supernatural omniscient entity may exist and I am happy with the concept that it does or does not. In my mind I am equal to any human on earth, yet the cosmos is a larger entity than my ego which is part of it. Human and possibly other sentient life forms can inject any meaning they like on the mutable perception of an external world and all without dogma are relevant to the individual being. To my mind's eye we are on Planet Earth to exist and live out a lifecycle and discover the inner man or spiritual aspect ourselves. I require no further meaning or understanding than this rather solipsistic insight. Philosophy is a nice little teaser, yet we are all less than specks of dust, mere minnows in what is in here and what is out there. In the last analysis I am without care.

SCIENCE

Science may depict causality

Model, theory, finality

Aiming to discover a world

Of objective, empirical reality

Yet it is a journey of the mind

External world it will not find

I saw the delusion of its claims

Since nature it will never tame.

RELIGION

We search for universal gods
Our beliefs all at odds
We build temples, churches, institutions
From prejudice, faith and fusions
Since primordial man, we have done what we can
Making sense of inner and outer spheres.
Hymns are music to our ears
The existence of gods we can refute
In argument, debate, dispute.

GOD OR DARWIN?

God and Darwin, both symbolic of man's
Enduring search for meaning and perhaps
An understanding of the origin of life
In the West, we search for a start
And finish, to the continuum, asking
Endless questions of science, religion
And other cultural norms
Embrace the notion that all just is,
Was and will be.
Humans trifle with their thoughts and
Beliefs, yet surely the mystic comes
Closest to the truth, and then, only
On a human perspective
We toy with fleeting images
Of the absolute.

JUNG

A scientist, mystic and visionary
Of thinking, intuition and feeling
He hit the psychic ceiling
Of archetype, shadow and wise man
He changed the face of space
And time that span
Living within his inner self
The books still fly off the shelf
In my humble opinion
He is a God of deep thinking tradition.

WILLIAM BLAKE

A master of the mystic
Not earthy, crude, realistic
He was a great genius,
Liberates, eases, and frees us
No user of deception
His extra-sensory perception
With primal force from subconscious
He penetrated way beyond us
Maestro of the fable
Disturbing and unstable
He saw the world in a grain of sand
And held infinity in the palm of his hand.

NIHILISM

If you insist
We do not exist
An abstraction of my mind
You think I am unkind
Prove to me the world has meaning
Beyond your reason and the scheming
While you all revel in solidarity
I am a nihilist, a human oddity
You see who is right and who is wrong
My little world view is my song.

FUTURE, PAST AND PRESENT

To my perceptive eye
No need to walk the path of timelessness
Beyond the word, God, eternity
The human face of sense of being
Is an ultimate oneness, embracing all possibilities
And notions of possibilities.
Do I create these words divorced from the great unknown
Or are these the echoes of a cunning ego?

HEAVEN

Heaven is a flight on the wings of euphoria
It is sweet embrace by the arms of ecstasy
Seduction by the light of the golden temple
Mystic realisation of selfhood
A pure essence of being beyond the word, the god, the world
It dwells in purity, at the core of beauty
The lover's sigh, wings of the butterfly
Nectar of the senses.

TIME

The ticking clock pulsates the rhythm of time

Created by the order of man

It is an interloper in the vastness of the cosmos

To bring structure to human chaos

Controlling, governing, having a human face in an unknown universe.

THE ABSOLUTE

The world of humanity

Is not one of clarity

It is relative, nebulous, unclear

Created by mind, instinct or fear

We try to perceive an outer world

Where all is clear, knowledge unfurled

Yet beyond the physical

Lurks a truth which is mystical

The ultimate journey of the soul

When the word and god become whole.

THE SELF

Take me on a kaleidoscope journey

To the centre of consciousness

to the far reaches of outer and inner space

To trace footsteps of the primordial man

Be at one with the cosmic whole

Take warmth from imagination's fire

Bask in the glory of uniqueness

Marvel at the divine beauty of the diamond,

The lotus, the archetype of archetypes

Leave a footprint in the sands of time.

THE COSMOS

The cosmos embraces our delusions that it can be known
The totality of science takes a miniscule place in the great web
All is one, one is all and thus it will be into space time and infinity
Beyond the word, science, god, is the immensity of ultimate reality
With vain delusion man seeks to know the unknowable
Since all he sees is his own reflection.

DOORS OF PERCEPTION

Open the doors, peel back the mind
Unleash the senses to the outer world
Do you see what I see, everyday reality,
Or are we all souls in a world of flux?
Probe deep
Search for what are the inner and outer realms
Layers of meaning can be perceived
Who's to say what is real and surreal?

IMMORTALITY

The urge for perpetual life
Is the origin of much strife
To conquer all infinity
Beyond the God, the Trinity.
It is a human convention
Of mind and conscious reflection
To beat the passage of time
Beyond the holy divine
Perhaps our aim is eternal fame
Before the final snuff
Of our worldly flame.

FROM ANOTHER PLACE

Sometimes I tap the depths of my feelings, in the well of being

They flow from another place, myself

As an instrument of a deep emotional orchestra of the mind

The thinker does not know the pure crystal beauty

that resonates from the font of holy people who failed to tap
the well of truth,

alienated from reality

A true poet speaks from the heart which is the source of
existential life itself.

GREATER THAN THYSELF

The moon, the giant orb, makes me wonder at my place

on this little dot, the Earth Mother

Giant egos, less than an ant, jostle in human juxtaposition

Living their dreams, nurturing fantasies, collective delusions

Bathed in ignorance, the collective voice of humanity is almost mute

Nebulous in the vastness of the time-space continuum

With consummate arrogance science attempts to capture reality

Yet is tainted by the sheer power of human bias

Mystics relish in an inner perception of human truth

So powerful, so simple, so Eastern in form.

ILLUSION, OR SUBJECTIVE REALITY?

It is simple, as to myself what I experience in my own psyche is a form
of conscious reality. As a writer and poet my own introspective
processes are the source of my creativity, since I work from within. It
sounds like introversion or solipsism, yet to me it is real. However,
there is a belief that we all live under a cloak of illusion, including
students of psychology who attempt to define the impact of the physical
brain. To my mind it is illusion to pretend or believe that people have
absolute knowledge of anything in the inner or outer worlds, under the

delusion of dogma. The gifted Mensan makes a shallow ripple on the ocean of truth. Discuss and analyse whether or not you can escape illusion.

THE DELUSION OF HUMAN DOGMA

Millions of people assert their opinions and beliefs in a distinctly human way. Right or wrong dissolves into verbal relativity. I have found that the conventions of culture are meaningful only if they are compatible with my personal experiences as a being on Planet Earth, or in the cosmos. This is me being dogmatic about what has meaning to my psyche. It feels fundamental for people to have belief systems and needs to aim for a response to and a perception of the external world as seen from a personal perspective. My belief informs me that I am content with the notion that my knowledge is zero of anything in a total and absolute sense; this helps to put the conscious ego in its place.

TRUTH

Truth can be treated as an abstract, philosophical concept, analysed by many intellectuals representing different belief systems, cultures and traditions. All of these are based in the psyche of man and carry human bias. I do not look outside in books, the external world for answers. Absolutes can be theoretical concepts. After years of thinking, I realise, from personal insight, that my personal perception of truth lies within myself. I take a subjective view when I ponder the world, the cosmos and all that I sense, perceive, intuit, feel and think. I am content with my findings in a microcosm within the macrocosm of complexity.

AWE AND LOSS OF CONSCIOUS EGO

In my time on Planet Earth I have felt a profound union with nature in forests, mountains, deserts and seas; all in the great outdoors. At times, on the edge of survival there has been the surge of primal, survival instincts. Lake Dahl in Kashmir was like an image of paradise, and the Golden Temple truly enchanting. In Nepal, whilst ruminating in scented gardens for the blind, Annapurna looked down on the miniscule being which was little man me. The presence of the mountains generated feelings of awe so that the conscious I dissolved into one beautiful feeling of cosmic connect. You perceive it as pure spirit, and it can be described as a mystical experience. On reflection, moments like this are life enhancing.

MIND'S LABYRINTH

In the depths of swirling emotions, I like things sharp and clear to satisfy the brain. My mind is hungry for clarity of thought in an ephemeral world of nebulous impressions. The gentle drift of the conscious self is both beautiful and wondrous, a finely-tuned instrument to cherish and revere. In all the souls of humanity at large, I continue with my private orchestra in the labyrinth of my mind. When the final curtain descends, I know that I will have found a friend, within my head.

EXPERIENCE AND INSIGHT

Time and age yield true perception and understanding of many aspects of life. I have met and studied many people, and the animals, plants and birds that make up life. They all have their lives to lead in the endless struggle for survival and to add to the next generation of life forms on Planet Earth. In the roles I have played in my career, the places seen and the characters met, lessons have been learned. The integrity of the inner man is vital, as society is ephemeral and in constant flux.

I am perceptive of the spiritual nature evident in much of humanity, and the individual personalities of birds and animals. Insight in this direction adds to the richness and complexity of life, and esoteric knowledge is a great survival tool.

Jung wrote of the archetype of the sage or wise man, and in the twilight of my life I cling to this concept and central tenet of his wisdom and belief system. I feel that penetrating insight gives true understanding towards the inner nature of things, and into the great questions that face thinking man, dreamers and mystics.

THE VISIONARY

Insight, foresight and prophecy are the realm of this cerebral genius. A child of unconvention, he illuminates his interests with creative gifts. I feel changes of consciousness and cultural perceptions are his legacy in the mainstream of the day. A radical and rebel against the established order, he leaves a singular footprint of true identity and individuality. These individuals are the new face of the arts and every walk of life where the power of intuition is felt.

THE RATIONAL INTELLECT AND CREATIVITY

Intellectuals tend to use sound logical thought processes, and may be deep thinking, analytical and perhaps philosophical. Academics assemble thousands of words, and with serious integrity towards convention and popular ideas of the day. As a poet and creative writer, I would ditch it all, the tedious formality, for one lovely poem, fresh from the deep brain that makes you laugh or cry; emotion can be more powerful than logic and reason, which I feel comes from the top of the psyche.

OBJECTIVITY

In human consciousness, some people refer to subjectivity and objectivity and separate the subject from the object. In psychological terms, this may assume an internal psyche separated from an external world of otherness or the cosmos as used in language. Man can hold a perception that all is one in a total fusion of everything that exists. This can be experienced as an intuitive feeling of unity or mysticism with little or no conscious perception of the separate id or ego. I feel this to be the case with the creation of some poetry or abstract ideas. Not every person will experience this state of being. It may happen when the external stimuli of the world are overwhelming to the senses and the brain, ie the impact on the inner man. It has happened to me in wilderness, mountains, seas and on the edge of survival. On reflection and in the cold light of day, the residue is of a spiritual nature, after the euphoria has subsided. You can then, experience nothing but subjectivity akin to solipsism.

WHAT WE KNOW OF THE COSMOS

I perceive that human consciousness is a part of the make-up of what we call the cosmos, that is all the entities, possible universes and dimensions that make up everything that can be conceived by all human minds, in regard to all that we regard as being out there. If we accept that the microcosm of human consciousness is a limited tool in the search for absolute knowledge of anything, which I do, then why persist in the delusion and foolish arrogance that science or any other discipline knows the answers to the nature and absolute understanding of universes and the cosmos? I am happy with my personal insight that everything just *is*, although accepting the idea that an omniscient entity may exist.

In subjective reality, on a personal level, I accept my ignorance and believe that some modern men are naïve to believe in or pursue knowledge of absolute reality, which to me is nebulous and beyond human comprehension - down to the curiosity of man I feel.

V

OTHER MATTERS

THE CAR'S THE STAR

I'm in love with a little tin god
Now I'm worldly, minted and odd
Shiny, red and starry
A spanking Enzo Ferrari
Out in repose and up for a pose
I drive along through York and Hull
I beautiful bird, I think I will pull
Polishing the bodywork every day
Insurance I sure will have to pay
It is my world, I cannot wait
To jump inside the driver's gate
With every fibre of my bottle
I race it when I press the throttle.

THE FAST LANE

I drop my tab, take my line
You, babe, will be real fine
One of the ultra-slick smarties
I go to the very best parties
Up with all the trends
And full of means to ends
I wear the latest designs
And never pay my fines
I studied at Oxbridge
Quails eggs, caviare in the fridge
Chatting to Gary Barlow
In the casino at Monte Carlo
Educated at the Sorbonne
I really am far gone.

THINGS AIN'T WHAT THEY USED TO BE

Now I'm a little older, I see through eyes of nostalgia
I remember Anna when things just cost a tanner
Politicians are so slick
They really make me sick
We like to show what we've all got,
Now things they really cost a lot
I used to go out and dance
Take holidays in the south of France
Now that everyone's on the take
I just sit and moan and ache
Used to feel so wild and free
Now things ain't what they used to be.

POETRY

Poetry takes its many forms
Way above the verbal norms
It aims to project the inner man
Into the book, the page, the scan
Resting in archives, vaults and tomes
Examples of its spiritual homes
Articulate thoughts and feelings bright
The poet knows what fits just right.

DIRTY DANCING

How I love dirty dancing
Snaking my hips and romancing
Being Mr Cool
All the ladies they just drool
I skip the light fandango

Music played on my banjo
Swaying and flowing across the floor
Opening every single door
Body lithe and full of tension
Master of every perception
I am a delight for hungry eyes
My six-pack ripples along with my thighs
It is the single dance of love
A gift from the Lord up above.

SLEEP

I close my eyes and enter another world
Far from constraints of wakefulness, I fly through the air
Sense a riot of colours, of strange forms and wonderful things
My dreams are signs of a vivid world
All is possible, every desire fulfilled
and when I wake shall I enter what is real, or is this an illusion?

THE OLD ROGUE

Full of syphilis, and emerging from the chrysalis
He admired the spiraea, racked with diarrhoea
In the garden of love
Where full of old scrap
He would enjoy a good crap
Sweet-scented phlox to sooth his pulsating pox
Memories of whores by the score
In rose-scented amour
After a lustful old life
He now pays the price
A life of lust, love, charm and abandon
The roguish old stallion.

SAVE THE PLANET

We have a moral duty
To save the world of beauty
All the creatures of distinction
On the verge of distinction
We have plundered Earth's resources
Its rivers, seas, and watercourses
Will man ever learn
Earth's wisdom not to spurn
To learn beauty and adore
Amazonian, hyacinthine macaw?
The world, its population
Will lead to more degradation
This is my final plea
The very last degree
Conquer the excess of materialism
And restore more apt idealism.

THE GARDENER

In years gone by Bill and Ben took my eye
From what I'd seen, my childhood dream
Would be the feared man who led from the potting shed
And with so much dread
Now I take my ease, as I study bees
In the calming luxuriance of my botanical heaven
Like a Taoist monk
My being is cemented in the florid beauty of my plantings
The soft earth embellished
By sweet Monet impressions
A feast of flora

Harmony to my senses
Cure for my defences.

CHOCOLATE

Each sensuous beautiful morsel caresses my lips
Heaven at my fingertips
Full power on
I absorb each divine moment
With the fullness of my being
The euphoria of my senses
As I engage in sweet embrace
With each sublime portion
Of Earthly pleasure
I give grace to Mother Nature for the gift.

DRUGS

Drugs to make me fly right across the sky
Those that calm me down
Take away the frown
You are under the spell
Doors of perception, heaven and hell
The world of every society
Is fixed by drugs so mighty
Even when you think you are clean
Influenced by another scheme
You need to get high
To reach, you and I
We party in inner space
Echoes of the human race.

TALENT

Let exquisite form stand above the norm
Sing your song, write more words
Bring joy to the hearts of men
Serve them with a fountain pen
Feel the rapture, taste the applause
You are the one, you are the cause
Now you've made it, you are a star
A shining light from near and far.

THE ALIEN

I am the creature from inner and outer space
Coming to stake my earthly place
Transmuting, transforming, leaving minds storming
I am beyond man's greatest invention
The product of another dimension.
I lurk in unknown places
Changing form, evolving faces
I am from beyond the stars
Further than Venus and Mars.

SOUNDS

Sounds that echo from my heart
Never keeping us apart
That play tunes with my feelings
Raise my spirit to the ceilings
They travel space and time
Our being to refine
The world is made profound
By every little sound
What music the savant must hear
On his violin of cheer.

THE WARLOCK

I am the witch, the master of spells
I come from the dark depths of hell
Here to haunt you and taunt you
To take your soul, to blow your mind
Leaving not a trace behind.
I am the magician, the mighty king
Sure to make your heart sing
Take away your gladness
Fill your mind with badness
And lead you to eternal damnation.

VOODOO WOMAN

I will seduce you with my charms
Break your little heart
Tear your soul apart
Fill you with fright
Shut out your light
Take you, make you and forsake you
I will consume you with my lust
and fill your brain with dust
The gypsy, I go unseen
Knower of all, the acid queen
I will fill you with desire
Show you my eternal fire
The voodoo woman comes to claim you
Kill your soul and make you
Into a living zombie now.

SWAN SONG

Moment of glory, the finest hour
Feel the rapture, sense the power
Final concerto of sweet music
Rush of feeling, sublime, orgasmic
Dreamed of these moments all along
I praise dear God and sing my song
Escape my body and learn to fly
Like a golden eagle in the sky.
Pulsating rhythm the heart strings tug
I'm flying on a beautiful wonder drug
The final rush of the whooper swan
In bursts of wonderful crescendo.

THE VIRUS

I lurk as microscopic death
Your very flesh to infect
Eating out your soul with maleficent evil
Here to take you on a voyage of despair
The miniscule torturer
Worshipping at the bosom of infection
Consumer of my giant host
The helpless human of doom.

APNOEA

Sleep broken by little starts
Alerting my mind to the moment
It was a subterranean landscape of fantasies
Layer upon layer of self-streaming
Springs into another dawn of daily events.

In the frozen time when breathing stops,
A sense of the rehearsal
The termination of life on Earth
It is another dent to my hopes
Of happiness and lasting contentment
The burden of life as a human.

CHEERFUL TODAY

Some may say I'm sanguine today
My cheeks are all rosy
Flushed warm and bright as a posy
Awakened from my stupor
Full of charm and good humour.
Life never dull
My little glass is fullness
Of warmth and understanding
My happiness strong and commanding
Feeling jovial, slick and quite hip
Must not let myself slide and slip.

TRUTH

The truth is my mistress
Penetrating, piercing the fog of deception
Bringer of joy to my introspection
Blessed by the God Almighty
The centre of my psyche.
She yields hope to my worldly system
The heart of my spiritual wisdom
Opens every page
On my journey to the sage.

PLACEBO

I take a little placebo
To cure my deflated ego
My mind is so robotic
Nervous, sensitive, neurotic
No longer feeling so ill
After my little pill
I am never bored
Happy now, completely cured
The sugar without description
Was an NHS prescription.

BIG BROTHER/PLASTIC T

I am colourful, humorous and unique.

My most unusual personality will be stimulating for the viewers.

I will add that extra something you want to see to the many team games and activities of the show.

In my home town I am known as a one-off character of repute.

WHO IS PROFESSOR JIM?

He is the light of introspection, ego, mind, reflection
With insight so superior
He penetrates interior
The spirit does not alter
Transcending every altar
Master of unconscious
Shadow, image, subconscious
His self is not effacing
With knowledge all-embracing
Sensitive to any stigma
That may tarnish his enigma
(Title by Rod Carter)

FEMININE MYSTIQUE

In my male mind
A lady I find
Alluring, charming and round
In nature not to be found
Complex, emotional, ethereal
A spiritual butterfly
That flits over the flowers of being
The perfect form is a union of the spiritual norm
Passing through life as one beautiful whole
(Dedicated to Jean)

HELL

Let us take a journey into despair
To a place where the mind is void
Taste the fiery heat of insanity
Fly on the wings of delusion
Find solace in a scream
Be consumed by unconscious force
Lose ourselves in the empty sea of humanity
Fall into the dark shadow
Never to return to the light of day.

PIGEONS

Pigeons are the end game
They bring me joy, they bring me fame
Gentle and without deception
And central to my perception
The fame of Barcelona dream
A product of my scheme

Has set the world on fire
Pinnacle of my desire
All the effort I can
Has made him known in Japan
From humble beginnings begun
I learned how to run and run
It was the apple of my eye
When I learned how to fly
Always on the pace
Master of the pigeon race.

BARCELONA INTERNATIONAL

A mistress, my obsession
Need to feel it a possession
So hot it gives me blisters
Fires my soul, it whispers
Perfection to my senses
Each heartbeat, emotion tenses
The Godhead, Lord Supreme
A world's best beauty queen
A mountain of the racing world
Pure magic not unfurled
Why not race from so very far
Become a racing superstar?

SUNSET

I sensed it, felt it, absorbed it
The beautiful golden orb
Takes its permanent place in my memory
An enduring taste of Goan sunshine

The hooded crow, a spectre of rich blackness
Flew, a silhouette across the face of the solar star
I would not return to this place
Yet would bask in sublime and beautiful images.

GHOSTS

I am the ghostly form
Way beyond the material norm
Walking through walls, houses and halls
Beyond imagination, wispy and fascinating
I am the paranormal
Ethereal and informal
A phantom of your psyche
Reality or might be
I am the spectre
Perceived by sensory perceptor
Flowing through time and space
To haunt the human race
In the deepest psyche I dwell
A remnant of an ancient hell.

MOONHEAD

I am the man in the moon
Here to take you out of your gloom
Shining down from very far
For you to gaze upon my star.
Wolves stand and howl at night
This will give you all a fright
Mountains crumble, slip and slide
While I affect the wind and tide

You know that I am here to stay
A lunar man, a great big ray
The sun and earth I am their friend
To shine and shine, eternal trend.

WADIRUM

Who has walked where Lawrence trod
The fierce sun scorching down on the empty quarter
I dared to take a look into the sandy cauldron
Not a place for white men
The shifting sands are born of time
Of searing winds, scorpions and desolation
Bedouins may conquer this hell
But not a white man in a city suit.

BAMIYAN

Deep, remote within the rugged mountains of the Hindu Kush
Mighty statues of Buddha stood
Monuments to faith and belief
They stared out to see pastel shades of the rich mountains
Now violated, destroyed by aggressive men
Acts by the ruthless Taliban.
I sat above the larger one
Gazing with wonder at timeless Afghanistan.

THE FLOODS OF YORK

Just when I thought I was floating along, the clouds did open, on the
happy throng.
The defences were not complete, the old systems now obsolete
It sharpened our senses, alerted our brains, as the floods encroached

from archaic drains
The human cost was great of trauma, sorry and hate
In the receding shallows I thought of the fate
Of man, who does what he can in the hands of a life span.

DELUSIONS

I'm going to win The X Factor
To fame, applause and rapture
Popular, rich and famous
All the world will name us.
I'm not ordinary, down to earth
The second coming of supreme birth
I am Jesus, God, an angel
The centre of a fable
The master of complex verse
Centre of the universe.

LIVING IN THE PAST

I go back ages
Faces, memories and pages
Recalling when I was wild
A wayward little child
I climb right up the stairs
In my very best flares
Wandering wild and free
In nature's womb was me
My parents tried to tame me
Discipline, control and make me
Yet I was one and singular
In the woods I honed my craft

The howling wind, but not yet daft
Now withdrawing from flux of life
Sharing the past with no known strife.

TRIPS

Walking in the harbour
Day out in sunny Scarborough
We are all so jolly
Full of life without a folly
We give the waiters tips
For our lovely fish and chips
All for one within our throng
As we sing our little song
Looking out towards the sea
Counting waves, one, two, three
We all assemble each of us
Back on this lovely little bus
It has been a great day out
All because it cost us nowt.

CHRISTMAS DAY

No slave to craze and convention, I hope to enjoy the feast of my
creative imagination. I shall take a step outside and linger a while in
the cold light of day, where the snowdrop blooms from the wintry
gloom, and the dove flies in the murky sky. Good humour I hope to find
in the spirit of mankind, and the light of true inspiration. I want it to
be a special day to dispel the ghosts of yesterday, when life was cold
and bleak, of things I dare not speak. The young ones in my clan will
bring warmth to an old man, who likes it pure and simple and to hear
the bells of truth on Christmas Day.

BOXING DAY

Yesterday when I was young and felt so strong

I was out with dog and gun

Under an ice crystal sun

Beyond the shroud, the foreboding crowd

I dwelt in hedgerows, barley stubble and meadows

Where rabbits lived and pheasants hid to escape the lonely hunter.

I came alive on the earthy clod and felt the power of the cosmic flow

That coursed energy from deep below.

It is good to tap the primal self that fuels the mind with the oxygen of insight.

And now alone in the rain-sodden gloom

I recall when my youth was in full bloom.

THE DEVILS OF DOOM

From the outer depths of hell

We cast our spell

For heartache and pain is the name of our game.

We eat into your brain

As you fall insane

Into the empty shadows of doom.

Not of madness, we are ancient spirits from the past,

A world of unconscious darkness, of dancing demons, the living dead

Where only evil was said

As the red-eyed goat bared gnarled and twisted horns.

Best to play in the light of day, a spiritual tune in a shimmering moon.

TESTING IN EDUCATION

I feel testing is necessary to discover the potential and identify some of the talents and capabilities of the children in support of the teaching methods and effectiveness of individual teachers and establishments. Overall I and many others have done well on it. There are problems with stresses generated by the system, and some people will show emotional and other psychological problems in the process. Systems change and evolve, yet thousands of creative and academic adults emerge to function in society.

Akin to the work of Steiner in anthroposophy, I do like to see the teaching and learning of morals and ethics, humanitarian and spiritual values. To be effective, great onus is placed on the ethos of the school to encourage children to function at a high level of consciousness. I am keen to cultivate the gifted, the very bright, and all pupils as a general idea.

A HUMANITARIAN APPROACH TO SPORTSMANSHIP

Rather than negate and denigrate the winners in the various competitive fields of endeavour, I feel that due recognition should be awarded to the best of their times and the champions as they impress themselves on the popular consciousness of the day. Intense emotions are aroused by the cauldron of competition, which are often manifested as jealousy and resentment - I have been guilty myself of this human frailty. People like the underdog, novelty and refreshing change to brighten up the day.

Man is a deeply psychological creature, and it is the psyche that creates the spiritual, humanitarian approach to the personality. These are noble ideas, and a more realistic approach may reveal the primal, dog-eat-dog approach to sportsmanship.

The need to forge and identity and prevail in the larger society is linked to the craving for fame. Outsiders in the media do celebrate the results of others, when respect by fellow members of the peer group is deeply felt. I tend to take a lofty, idealistic view of things.

MAINTAINING THE DREAM

Great ideas come and go with the general flow. When you realise a dream and make it a concrete reality, try and replace it with another one. In this sense you will have aspirations, hopes and expectations to give an edge and a meaning to life. This is a personal, individual, subjective approach and is fed by the brain. It is important to make the right connections with people and influences from a constantly changing world, of nature, people and things.

In my life I have changed ambitions as they come and go, to keep stimulated, fresh and alive. Little targets each day feed the buzz of gentle excitement that drives you on to self-realisation. One of the most lovely insects to behold is the industrious bumble bee, as it lives out its innocuous and worthy little life, a fine example from the wonderful world of nature.

NOSTALGIA

In the early sixties, and living in Gilbert Street, Alvaston, Derby, I flew a nice little kit of rollers after school. It was the highlight of my day watching them fly and spin, and I learned everyone in the air. Now the Murphins lived in the same area, with racers. They told me off for flying the kit on a race day. Presently I was round at the dad's loft, sitting watching the racers come home, like Chunky and Young Chunky. I enjoyed the quiet, patient life and was hooked on the gentle ways of the elder Mr Murphin. The seeds of my future career were sown. The lads had a Vauxhall Velox with column change that looked stylish.

It is very important that you meet people of good influence in life. Where pigeons of all types flew in Derby, I was round at the lofts to learn all about them. There was old Harold Adams, Billy Burdett, Frank Bryant and Graham Dexter, and I have fond, formative memories of all these characters.

STARS

Speeding through the universe, we are stars, we are dust

In infinity we trust.

To ride on a comet, dance on the moon,

To hear the sound, whistle the tune.

The wondrous story as the cosmos unfolds, to travel light, beyond space and time

To other dimensions that we will find.

We are beyond the minds of men

Imagination of quill and pen.

Our spirits have been unleashed

To soar and float in reaches way beyond the human race.

This is my hour, it is my life, an enchanting journey to the stars.

ICE MAN

He is so cool, the man with the ice in the eyes. Like a wolf in tundra, the air that he breathes is of snowflakes and crystals that sparkle in the Arctic sun. Detached, aloof in touch with primal elements, he walks alone in tandem with the earth, the sun, the moon and the stars. The soul is deep, beyond the scope of common man, made rich and whole by a life on the edge and in the fire of experience.

Our iceman, an enigma, walks alone and cannot be known by men who live in blind acceptance of the norm. What grace and beauty are to be found in this man, so profound?

THE GIRL AND THE SHADOW

The little girl watched aglow

At the shadow she was coming to know.

The stranger skipped and danced, alerting her trance

And mirrored her every move.

In a voice soft and sweet, she gave Granddad a treat

As the shadow came alive in the imagination of her eyes.

She loved him so, who was charmed to know

That her invisible friend was well on the mend, and having fun with them too.

A HIGHER PLACE

Rise up to a higher place, the lofty peak of the human race

Soar like an eagle and sing like a lark, no more alone in the dark

Hear the music of the spheres as it soothes my inner ears

In this place I stand alone in the power of the transcendence zone

It is my yen to keep the Zen and capture pure feelings of rapture

beyond the clouds that obscure my sight, floating as an angel in pure starlight.

I want to feel wild and free in the heart and pulse of destiny.

Why should I fall back to Earth

When there is a higher place, and heaven awaits my newborn faith?

A WALK ON THE WILD SIDE

Strip off those conventions, discard the cares and squeeze the juice out of life itself. Sense the wind of change and bask in freedom, the gentle rain and the warm summer breeze. This trip is a one-way ticket, a vast intoxicating encounter and a single experiment in being. It may take you to the far edge of experience, to see the rising sun at the roof of the world, to be kissed by ocean currents as exotic fish fill the senses in a myriad of shapes, colours and diversity. This is your one and only chance on Planet Earth, welcome it, embrace it and take a walk on the wild side.

www.ingramcontent.com/pod-product-compliance
Lightning Source LLC
Chambersburg PA
CBHW060031050426
42448CB00012B/2956